Franz LISZT

Héroïde Funèbre
Symphonic Poem No. 8
S. 102

Study Score
Partitur

PETRUCCI LIBRARY PRESS

INTRODUCTION

The present score is a reissue of one from the Franz Liszt-Stiftung edition, originally published by Breitkopf & Härtel from 1907-1936. The edition was prepared in an effort to publish the entire oeuvre of Franz Liszt. Editors included such prominent musicians as Béla Bartok, Ferruccio Busoni, Eugène d'Albert and José Vianna da Motta – some of whom studied with Liszt – as well as scholars like Peter Raabe, who would later compile the first catalog of the composer's works. The need for a complete edition was already apparent by the time of Liszt's death. Although some of his piano music had regularly appeared in new editions throughout his life, these works were by no means representative of even his pianistic output. A far more unfortunate fate was left for his orchestral music - which would usually be issued only once, soon to go out of print and later scarcely available. The Liszt-Stiftung edition revived many works that had fallen into relative obscurity and was therefore handsomely welcomed.

The edition was sadly never completed. The publication activity was brought to a premature end by the time of the Second World War. All in all the incomplete edition encompassed 34 volumes, among others two symphonies, the symphonic poems, some concert works, a couple of piano arrangements and 11 volumes of original works for piano – a mere fraction of the composer's output – but the edition would nonetheless break the ground for Liszt research during the 20th century for a number of reasons. First, it brought to light a number of late pieces that would put Liszt as a forerunner of experimental music and firmly establish his position as such. Second, it revealed the diversity of Liszt's output, which up until that time had been best known as an important addition to the piano repertoire. Third, it displayed the complex and characteristic nature of many of his works by being the first edition to show and make use of several alternative (sometimes vastly different) versions and sources. Last but not least, it would provide the world with a generally reliable edition of easy availability and very high standard for its day.

The Bavarian State Library acquired a complete copy of said edition and decided to digitize it in 2008. By that time more than 70 years had passed since its publication, effectively rendering the edition out of copyright and free for any use. Each and every page was scanned and uploaded to their online digital collection. While this was a great effort in itself, the site has a rudimentary interface, is difficult to navigate and the scores are not in the context of relevant information. One of our users decided to also upload it to our site, the International Music Score Library Project (IMSLP) / Petrucci Music Library, the unique wiki-based repository of musical scores, composers and indexes that anyone can edit and amend. Through the effort of a single user, Mattias K. (piupianissimo), the entire edition is now easily

available worldwide to those who wish to perform and study the composer's music in a historical context, since as the case is with Liszt's music, many early editions exist and many are readily available on the site and many more will be available in the future. IMSLP is as such a valuable resource available to the scholar but even more to the performer who is always a mere mouse click away from scores that have not been in print since the turn of the past century, or that are otherwise hard to come by. The availability, quantity of ease of access for online scores will soon exceed those of the traditional medium of print. Nevertheless new works have always been published through the printed medium and this tradition is going to persist for many years to come even if complemented by the digital medium. Of course an important fact to stress is that the availability of digital scores online does not exclude the need of printed score since neither one can replace the comfort and neatness of one another. The quality of a bound reprint or new engraving exceeds that of a score printed at home.

I discovered IMSLP back in early 2006 when it first began. At that time many scores were scattered on the net either privately or on commercial collection sites. Many of these sites had a considerably large collection but sadly many had restrictions on number of downloads per day and the process of contributing to them was riddled with bureaucracy. IMSLP was the first free site where anyone could contribute and upload any kind of musical scores. I have personally searched and uploaded many works – particularly those of Liszt – and the future of the site is nothing but bright. At the time of its start only a handful of scores were available on the site but through the effort of its users IMSLP has grown to be the largest collection of scores available on the Internet.

Héroïde funèbre is the eighth work in a series of thirteen symphonic poems composed by Franz Liszt. It was composed from 1849-56 and first published in 1857 by Breitkopf und Härtel of Leipzig. The dedicatee is Princess Carolyne zu Sayn-Wittgenstein. This score is from the fourth volume of the Franz Liszt-Stiftung edition, edited by Otto Taubmann and published in 1909. The score, along with a number or arrangements, is also available directly at the following URL:
http:// imslp.org/wiki/Héroïde_funèbre,_S.102_(Liszt,_Franz)

Soren Afshar (Funper)
Summer, 2011

COMPOSER'S PREFACE

Eine Aufführung, welche den Intentionen des Komponisten entsprechen und ihnen Klang, Farbe, Rhythmus und Leben verleihen soll, wird bei meinen Orchester-Werken am zweckmässigsten und mit dem geringsten Zeitverlust durch geteilte Vor-Proben gefördert werden. Demzufolge erlaube ich mir, die HH. Dirigenten, welche meine symphonischen Dichtungen aufzuführen beabsichtigen, zu ersuchen, der General-Probe Separat-Proben mit dem Streich-Quartett, andere mit Blas- und Schlag-Instrumenten vorangehen zu lassen.

Gleichzeitig sei mir gestattet zu bemerken, dass ich das mechanische, taktmässige, zerschnittene Auf- und Abspielen, wie es an manchen Orten noch üblich ist, möglichst beseitigt wünsche, und nur den periodischen Vortrag, mit dem Hervortreten der besonderen Accente und der Abrundung der melodischen und rhythmischen Nuanzierung, als sachgemäss anerkennen kann. In der geistigen Auffassung des Dirigenten liegt der Lebensnerv einer symphonischen Produktion, vorausgesetzt, dass im Orchester die geziemenden Mittel zu deren Verwirklichung sich vorfinden; andernfalls möchte es ratsamer erscheinen, sich nicht mit Werken zu befassen, welche keineswegs eine Alltags-Popularität beanspruchen.

Obschon ich bemüht war, durch genaue Anzeichnungen meine Intentionen zu verdeutlichen, so verhehle ich doch nicht, dass Manches, ja sogar das Wesentlichste, sich nicht zu Papier bringen lässt, und nur durch das künstlerische Vermögen, durch sympathisch schwungvolles Reproduzieren, sowohl des Dirigenten als der Aufführenden, zur durchgreifenden Wirkung gelangen kann. Dem Wohlwollen meiner Kunstgenossen sei es daher überlassen, das Meiste und Vorzüglichste an meinen Werken zu vollbringen.

Weimar, März 1856.

Pour obtenir un résultat d'exécution correspondant aux intentions de mes œuvres orchestrales, et leur donner le coloris, le rhythme, l'accent et la vie qu'elles réclament, il sera utile d'en préparer la répétition générale par des répétitions partielles des instruments à cordes, à vent, en cuivre, et à percussion. Par cette méthode de la division du travail on épargnera du temps en facilitant aux exécutants l'intelligence de l'ouvrage. Je me permets en conséquence de prier MM. les chefs d'orchestre qui seraient disposés à faire exécuter l'un de ces Poèmes symphoniques, de vouloir bien prendre le soin de faire précéder les répétitions générales, des répétitions préalables indiquées ci-dessus.

En même temps j'observerai que la mesure dans les œuvres de ce genre demande à être maniée avec plus de mesure, de souplesse, et d'intelligence des effets de coloris, de rhythme, et d'expression qu'il n'est encore d'usage dans beaucoup d'orchestres. Il ne suffit pas qu'une composition soit régulièrement bâtonnée et machinalement exécutée avec plus ou moins de correction pour que l'auteur ait à se louer de cette façon de propagation de son œuvre, et puisse y reconnaître une fidèle interprétation de sa pensée. Le nerf vital d'une belle exécution symphonique gît principalement dans la compréhension de l'œuvre reproduite, que le chef d'orchestre doit surtout posséder et communiquer, dans la manière de partager et d'accentuer les périodes, d'accuser les contrastes tout en ménageant les transitions de veiller tantôt à établir l'équilibre entre les divers instruments, tantôt à les faire ressortir soit isolément soit par groupes, car à tel moment il convient d'entonner ou de marquer simplement les notes, mais à d'autres il s'agit de phraser, de chanter, et même de déclamer. C'est au chef qu'il appartient d'indiquer à chacun des membres de l'orchestre la signification du rôle qu'il a à remplir.

Je me suis attaché à rendre mes intentions par rapport aux nuances, à l'accélération et au retard des mouvements, etc. aussi sensibles que possible par un emploi détaillé des signes et des expressions usitées; néanmoins ce serait une illusion de croire qu'on puisse fixer sur le papier ce qui fait la beauté et le caractère de l'exécution. Le talent et l'inspiration des artistes dirigeants et exécutants en ont seuls le secret, et la part de sympathie que ceux-ci voudront bien accorder à mes œuvres, seront pour elles le meilleur gage de succès.

Weimar, Mars 1856.

In order to secure a performance of my orchestral works which accords with their intentions, and which imparts to them the colour, rhythm, accent and life that they require, it is recommended that the general rehearsal should be preceded by separate rehearsals of the Strings, Wind, Brass, and instruments of percussion. By this division of labour time will be saved, and the executants will more rapidly be made familiar with what is required of them. I therefore venture to request that conductors, who are pleased to bring one or the other of my symphonic poems to a hearing will adopt the plan formulated above.

At the same time I may be allowed to remark that it is my wish that the mechanical, bar by bar, up and down beating of time, which obtains in so many places, should as far as possible be discarded, and that only the periodic divisions, with the prominence of certain accentuation and the rounding off of melodic and rhythmical nuances should alone be regarded as indispensable. The vitality of a symphonic performance depends upon the intellectual perception of the conductor, presuming that suitable material for its realisation is to be found in the orchestra; failing this it would seem to be advisable to hold aloof from works which do not claim a promise of every-day popularity.

Although I have endeavoured to make my intentions clear by providing exact marks of expression, I cannot conceal from myself that much, and that perhaps the most important, cannot be set forth on paper, but can only be successfully brought to light by the artistic capability and the sympathetic and enthusiastic reproduction by both conductor and executants. It may therefore be left to my colleagues in art to do the most and best that they can for my works.

Weimar, March 1856.

F. Liszt.

HELDENKLAGE.

SYMPHONISCHE DICHTUNG Nr. 8 VON F. LISZT.

Man hat mehrfach von einer Symphonie gesprochen, welche wir im Jahre 1830 komponiert haben. Verschiedene Gründe haben uns veranlasst, sie im Portefeuille zu bewahren. Indem wir aber diese Reihe von symphonischen Dichtungen veröffentlichen, fügen wir ein Fragment jenes Werkes, den ersten Teil desselben, bei. —

Der menschliche Geist, weit entfernt, in grösserer Stabilität zu verharren, als die übrige Natur, erscheint im Gegenteil beweglicher als irgend etwas. Wie man auch seine beständige Tätigkeit bezeichnen möge, als fortschreitende Entwicklung, als spiralförmige Bewegung oder als einfachen Kreislauf, so steht eines immer fest: dass er bei Völkern wie bei Individuen niemals gänzlichem Stagnieren anheimfällt. In stetem Wechsel erscheinen und vergehen die Dinge wie ein Traum, wie die Wellen einer ewig zu den Küsten der Jahrhunderte emporschwellenden Flut, so dass einerseits die Ansichten unaufhörlich sich ändern, wir andrerseits sie verschieden auffassen. Dieser zweifache Impuls hat zur Folge, dass viele Gesichtspunkte in unsrer geistigen Anschauung notwendig sich verändern, dass unser Verstand sie in sehr verschiedene Rahmen fasst, dass sie in unserem Geiste in durchaus veränderten Färbungen sich wiederspiegeln. Von dieser unaufhörlichen Umwandlung der Gegenstände und Eindrücke sind aber einige ausgenommen, welche jeden Wechsel überdauern, welche ihrer Natur nach unveränderlich sind. So unter andern und vor allem der Schmerz, dessen finstre Gegenwart uns immer denselben Schauer einflösst, und zu ehrerbietigem Beugen zwingt, uns sympathisch anzieht, während er uns mit Schrecken erfüllt, uns immer gleiches Beben empfinden lässt, suche er nun Gute oder Böse, Sieger oder Besiegte, Weise oder Sinnlose, Mächtige oder Schwache heim. In welchem Herzen, auf welchem Boden er immer seine giftschwangere Vegetation ausbreiten möge, woher er stamme, welches sein Ursprung sei, sobald er in seiner wahrhaften Grösse vor uns steht, ist er erhaben und erheischt unsere Ehrfurcht. Aus zwei feindlichen Lagern hervorgegangen und rauchend von jüngst vergossnem Blut, erkennen die Schmerzen sich als Sprossen desselben Stammes; sie sind die schicksalwaltenden unabwendbaren Schnitter jedes Stolzes, die unerbittlichen Ebner aller Geschicke. Alles ist in der menschlichen Gesellschaft dem Wechsel untertan, Sitte und Kultus, Gesetze und Ideen: der Schmerz bleibt stets ein und derselbe, wie er es seit dem Anfangs der Dinge gewesen ist. Reiche wer-

HÉROÏDE FUNÈBRE.

POÈME SYMPHONIQUE No. 8 DE F. LISZT.

On a parlé plusieurs fois d'une symphonie que nous avons composée en 1830. Diverses raisons nous ont engagé à la garder en portefeuille. Cependant, en publiant cette série de poèmes symphoniques, nous avons voulu y insérer un fragment de cet ouvrage, sa première partie.

L'esprit humain, loin d'être plus stable que le reste de la nature, nous apparaît au contraire plus mouvementé que quoi que ce soit. De quelque nom qu'on appelle sa constante activité, marche, progrès spiral, ou simplement révolution circulaire, toujours est-il constaté qu'il ne reste jamais stationnaire ni dans les peuples, ni dans les individus. De leur côté les choses, jamais immobiles, comme les vagues d'une marée éternellement montante sur la plage des siècles, avancent et passent; on dirait un songe. Ainsi d'une part, les aspects diffèrent sans cesse, de l'autre, nous ne les considérons plus de même. De cette double impulsion il résulte, que bien des points de vue changent nécessairement pour les yeux de notre esprit: celui-ci les embrasse dans les cadres divers, et ceux-là s'y réfléchissent sous des couleurs très dissemblables. Mais cette perpétuelle transformation d'objets et d'impressions, il en est qui survient à tous les changements, à toutes les mutations, et dont la nature est invariable. Telle entr'autres et surtout la Douleur, dont nous contemplons la morne présence toujours avec le même pâle recueillement, la même terreur secrète, le même respect sympathique et la même frémissante attraction, soit qu'elle visite les bons ou les méchants, les vaincus ou les vainqueurs, les sages ou les insensés, les forts ou les faibles. Quel que soit le cœur et le sol sur lesquels elle étend sa végétation funeste et vénéneuse, quelles que soient son extraction et son origine, sitôt qu'elle grandit de toute sa hauteur elle nous paraît auguste, elle impose la révérence. Sorties de deux camps ennemis, et fumantes encore d'un sang fraîchement versé, les douleurs se reconnaissent pour sœurs, car elles sont les fatidiques faucheuses de tous les orgueils, les grandes niveleuses de toutes les destinées. Tout peut changer dans les sociétés humaines, mœurs et cultes, lois et idées; la Douleur reste une même chose; elle reste ce qu'elle a été depuis le commencement des temps. Les empires croulent, les civilisations s'effacent, la science conquiert des mondes, l'intelligence humaine luit d'une lumière toujours plus intense; rien ne fait pâlir son intensité, rien ne la déplace du siège où elle règne en notre âme,

HEROIC ELEGY.

SYMPHONIC POEM No. 8 BY F. LISZT.

People have often spoken of a symphony which I composed in 1830. For many reasons I decided on keeping it in my portfolio. Nevertheless, on publishing this series of Symphonic Poems, I have thought well to include a fragment of this work, viz. its first movement.

The human mind far from being more stable than the rest of nature, on the contrary seems to be more changeable than anything else. By whatever term its constant activity, march, spiral progress, or merely circular revolution may be called, it is always to be found, that it never remains stationary either among people or individuals. On their side things ever immovable like the waves of an ever mounting tide on the shores of ages advance and pass; one might call it a dream. Thus on the one hand its aspects constantly change; on the other, we no longer consider them in the same way. The double result of this impulsion is that many points of view necessarily change for the eyes of our mind. The latter embrace them in different frames, and the former reflect them under very dissimilar colours. But in this perpetual transformation of objects and impressions there are those which survive all changes, all variations, and whose nature is unchangeable. Such, amongst others, and above all, is Grief, whose gloomy presence we regard always with the same wan contemplation, the same secret terror, the same sympathetic respect, and the same shuddering attraction, whether she visit the good, or the wicked, the vanquished, or the conquerors, the wise or the foolish, the strong or the feeble. Whatever may be the heart and the soil upon which she spreads her poisonous vegetation, whatever may be her extraction and her origin, as soon as she rises to all her greatness she appears to us august, she imposes reverence. Taking their origin from two opposing camps, and still reeking with blood recently shed, griefs recognise each other as sisters, because they are the fatal mowers of all pride, the great levellers of all destinies. Everything may change in human societies, manners, religions, laws, and ideas, but Grief remains the same, she remains what she has been since the beginning of time. Empires fall, civilisations die out, science conquers the world, human intelligence shines with an always more intense light, nothing displaces her from the seat where she reigns in our soul, nothing expels her from her privileges of eldership, nothing modifies her solemn and inexorable supremacy. Her tears are al-

den erschüttert, Civilisationen verblühen, die Wissenschaft erobert neue Welten, der menschliche Geist leuchtet stets intensiver — durch nichts aber wird die Intensität des Schmerzes gebleicht, durch nichts wird er von dem Sitz entthront, auf welchem er herrscht in unsrer Seele, nichts vermag ihm die Vorrechte der Erstgeburt zu entreissen, nichts mildert sein feierliches, unerbittliches Obwalten. Die Tränen, die er erzeugt, sind immer dasselbe bittere brennende Nass, sein Schluchzen moduliert immer in denselben durchschneidenden Tönen, mit unveränderlicher Monotonie pflanzt sein Verzagen sich fort. Seine dunkle Ader strömt durch alle Herzen und verbreitet unheilbare Wunden in ihnen. Über alle Zeiten und Orte weht sein Leichenpanier.

Wenn es uns gelungen ist, einige seiner Accente zu Klängen zu gestalten, das Kolorit seiner roten Finsternisse wiederzugeben, wenn wir vermocht haben, die Verheerung zu schildern, welche sich niedersenkt auf Trümmer, die Majestät, welche um verödete Ruinen schwebt, dem Schweigen eine Stimme zu leihen, das auf Katastrophen folgt, den Schrei des Entsetzens während Schreckensereignissen nachtönen zu machen, wenn wir die trüben Scenen erschaut und richtig erfasst haben, wie sie die, den Hingang einer alten Ordnung der Dinge oder das Entstehen einer neuen stets begleitende, allgemeine Not im Gefolge hat — so möchte unser Bild immer und überall als wahr befunden werden. Auf jener zweischneidigen Schwelle, welche jedes blutige Ereignis zwischen Vergangenheit und Zukunft stellt, bleiben Leid, Angst, Trauer und Leichenzüge immer und überall dieselben. In jede Siegesfanfare mischt sich immer und überall eine trübe Begleitung von Sterbeseufzern und Angstrufen, Gebeten und Lästerungen, gepresstem Schluchzen und Scheidegrüssen. Man möchte sagen, dass der Mensch mit triumphalen Kostümen und Festkleidern sich nur bedecke, um den Trauerflor zu verbergen, der wie ein Epiderm dicht verwachsen ist mit seiner sterblichen Hülle.

De Maistre bemerkt, dass man auf je Tausende von Jahren als seltne Ausnahmen nur einige rechnen kann, in welchen Frieden auf Erden herrschte, auf dieser Arena, wo Völker wie Gladiatoren sich bekämpfen und wo die Tapfersten, wenn sie in die Schranken treten, vor dem Schicksal als Meister und der Vorsehung als Schiedsrichter sich neigen. Welches auch die Farben der Fahnen sein mögen, welche in diesen gleich unheilvollen Spielen aufeinander folgenden Kriegen und Verwüstungen sich kühn und stolz in den feindlichen Lagern gegeneinander stellen — alle sind in Heldenblut, in unversiegbare Tränen getaucht. Da naht die Kunst und hüllt den Grabhügel der Tapfern in ihren schimmernden Schleier, und krönt Sterbende und Tote mit ihrer Glorie, auf dass ihr Los neidenswert sei vor den Lebenden.

rien ne l'expulse de ses privilèges de primogéniture, rien ne modifie sa solennelle et inexorable suprématie. Ses larmes sont toujours de la même eau amère et brûlante: ses sanglots sont toujours modulés sur les mêmes notes stridentes et lamentables; ses défaillances se perpétuent avec une inaltérable monotonie; sa veine noire court à travers chaque cœur, et son dard brûlant contagie chaque âme de quelque incurable blessure. Son étendard funéraire flotte sur tous les temps et tous les lieux.

Si nous avons su recueillir quelques-uns de ses accents, si nous avons saisi le sombre coloris de ses rouges ténèbres, si nous avons réussi à peindre la désolation qui s'abat sur les décombres et les majestés qui se répandent sur les ruines, à prêter une voix aux silences qui suivent les catastrophes, à répéter les cris effarés jetés durant les désastres; si nous avons bien écouté et bien entendu les lugubres scènes qui se jouent dans les calamités publiques produites par la mort ou la naissance d'un ordre de choses, un pareil tableau peut être vrai partout et toujours. Sur ce seuil tranchant que tout événement sanglant bâtit entre le passé et l'avenir, les souffrances, les angoisses, les regrets, les funérailles se ressemblent partout et toujours. Partout et toujours on entend sous les fanfares de la victoire, un sourd accompagnement de râles et de gémissements, d'oraisons et de blasphèmes, de soupirs et d'adieux, et l'on pourrait croire que l'homme ne revêt des manteaux de triomphe et des habits de fête, que pour cacher un deuil qu'il ne saurait dépouiller, comme s'il était un invisible épiderme.

De Maistre observe que sur des milliers d'années, c'est à peine si l'on en pourrait compter quelques-unes durant lesquelles, par rare exception, la paix régna sur cette terre, qui ressemble ainsi à une arène où les peuples se combattent comme jadis les gladiateurs, et où les plus valeureux en entrant en lice, saluent le Destin leur maître, et la Providence leur arbitre. Dans ses guerres et ces carnages qui se succèdent, sinistres jeux, quelle que soit la couleur des drapeaux qui se lèvent fiers et hardis l'un contre l'autre, sur les deux camps ils flottent trempés de sang héroïque et de larmes intarissables. A l'Art de jeter son voile transfigurant sur la tombe des vaillants, d'encercler de son nimbe d'or les morts et les mourants, pour qu'ils soient enviés des vivants.

F. Liszt.

ways of the same bitter and burning water: her sobs are always modulated upon the same harsh and lamentable notes; her swoons continue with unalterable monotony; her black poison circulates through each heart, and her burning dart infects each soul with some incurable wound. Her funeral banner floats upon all times and all places.

If we have known how to gather some of her accents, if we have seized the sombre colouring of her red darkness, if we have succeeded in painting the desolation which falls upon the heaps of rubbish and the majesties which spread themselves upon the ruins, in lending a voice to the silence which follows catastrophes, in repeating the wild cries uttered during disasters; if we have listened and heard well the mournful scenes enacted in the public calamities produced by the death or birth of an order of things, such a picture can be everywhere and always true. Upon this two-sided threshold which each bleeding event builds between the past and the future, sufferings, anguish, regrets, funerals are everywhere and always the same. Everywhere and always is heard among the trumpets of victory a low accompaniment of death-rattles, and of groans, of prayers and of blasphemies, of sighs and farewells, and one could believe that man only puts on the cloak of triumph and festal garments to hide a mourning which he did not know how to throw off, as if it were an invisible skin.

De Maistre observes that during thousands of years, only a few could be counted when by a rare exception, peace reigned upon this earth, which thus resembles an arena where people fight, as of old the gladiators did; and where the bravest in entering the lists salute Destiny as their master, and Providence as their arbitrator. In these wars, and massacres which follow each other, sinister games, whatever may be the colour of the flags which rise proud and daring one against the other, over the two camps, they float steeped in heroic blood and in inexhaustible tears. It is for art to throw her transfiguring veil upon the tomb of the brave, to encircle the dead and dying with her golden halo, so that they may be envied by the living.

After the 1854 relief by Ernst Rietschel

INSTRUMENTATION

2 Flutes
Piccolo
2 Oboes
English Horn
2 Clarinets
2 Bassoons

4 Horns
2 Trumpets
3 Trombones
Tuba

Timpani
Percussion
(Snare Drum, Bass Drum, Cymbals, Tam-Tam, 2 Chimes)

Violins I
Violins II
Violas
Violoncellos
Basses

Duration: ca. 20 minutes

First Performance: November 10, 1857
Breslau: Orchestra
Franz Liszt, conductor

ISBN: 978-1-60874-028-4

This score is an unabridged reprint of the score
first issued in Leipzig by Breitkopf & Härtel, 1909. Plate F.L. 8

Printed in the USA
First Printing: December, 2011

HÉROÏDE FUNÈBRE
Symphonic Poem No. 8
S. 102

FRANZ LISZT (1811–1886)

4

8

Der Buchstabe R.... bedeutet ein geringes Ritardando, so zu sagen: ein leises crescendo des Rhythmus.
The letter R.... signifies a slight Ritardando, so to speak: a gentle crescendo of the rhythm.
La lettre R.... signifie un petit Ritardando, c'est-à-dire: un doux crescendo du rhythme.

22

40284

24

25

26

38

*) Nicht tremolieren.
 Not a tremolo.
 Pas un trémolo.

*) Nicht tremolieren.
Not a tremolo.
Pas un trémolo.

40284

42

46

48

40284

FRANZ LISZTS SYMPHONISCHE DICHTUNGEN 7 u. 8

REVISIONSBERICHT

Im Jahre 1908 wurden in einer gemeinschaftlichen Sitzung der Revisoren, der Herausgeber und der Verleger die Leitgedanken und Grundsätze für eine vollständige, einheitliche und korrekte Gesamtausgabe der Werke Franz Liszts beraten und endgültig festgesetzt.

Aus praktischen Gründen der modernen Musikpflege mußten die vielfachen Unterschiede in der Benennung und Anordnung der Instrumente, in den Schlüsseln usw., vor allem aber sehr viele, für heutige Begriffe überflüssige oder selbst störende Versetzungszeichen beseitigt werden. Die auf letztere bezügliche Bestimmung lautet in endgültiger Fassung:

»Die von Liszt sehr reichlich angewendeten zufälligen Versetzungszeichen (namentlich Auflösungszeichen) sind für die heutige Praxis zum Teil entbehrlich geworden. Die nicht unbedingt notwendigen sind nur da beizubehalten, wo sie das Lesen tatsächlich noch erleichtern, Mißverständnisse verhüten oder für das harmonische Bild Lisztscher Schreibweise besonders charakteristisch erscheinen.«

Um jede Willkür auszuschliessen, sind alle irgendwie nennenswerten Änderungen, Weglassungen, Zusätze im Wortlaut der Lisztschen Partitur im Revisionsbericht je bei der betreffenden Komposition besonders aufgeführt und begründet worden, sodaß jeder mit der alten und der neuen Ausgabe in der Hand sich sein Urteil selbst bilden kann. Alle Zutaten, insbesondere Vortragsbezeichnungen, wurden in Klammern ( ) oder [ ] gesetzt; in einzelnen Fällen kann und soll dies nachträglich noch geschehen.

Die Herausgabe der Symphonischen Dichtungen war ursprünglich von Herrn Eugen d'Albert übernommen worden, der jedoch wegen anderweitiger großer Inanspruchnahme zurücktrat, nachdem er den Stich aller 12 Werke nur in erster Lesung hatte beaufsichtigen können. Die genaue Nachprüfung übernahm in dankenswerter Weise Herr Otto Taubmann in Berlin, in stetem Einvernehmen mit dem Kustos des Liszt-Museums, Herrn Hofrat Dr. Obrist, als dem Obmann der Revisionskommission.

BAND 4

FESTKLÄNGE.
Symphonische Dichtung Nr. 7.

Vorlage: 1. Die erste Partiturausgabe, erschienen 1856 bei Breitkopf & Härtel in Leipzig. Verlagsnummer 9120.

2. Die autographe Partitur im Liszt-Museum in Weimar.

3. Varianten, Kürzungen und Errata. Als Anhang zu den Festklängen 1861 bei Breitkopf & Härtel erschienen. Verlagsnummer 10176.

Bemerkungen:

S. 12. Die gedruckte Vorlage hat im 4. Takt für die Hörner eine zweifelhafte dynamische Vorschrift. Während 1. und 2. Horn (gleich den Holzbläsern) auf der ganzen Note ein Marcatozeichen (>) haben, fehlt dieses bei dem 3. und 4. Horn, bei denen statt dessen ein Crescendo-Zeichen (⟨) steht. Liszts Manuskript hat dieses Crescendo-Zeichen für alle vier Hörner. Vielleicht wollte er damit das »empor« der Trompetenfanfare unterstützen, während die Holzbläser nur abschließen sollen.

* * *

HÉROÏDE FUNÈBRE.
Symphonische Dichtung Nr. 8.

Vorlage: Die erste Partiturausgabe, erschienen 1857 bei Breitkopf & Härtel in Leipzig. Verlagsnummer 9318.

Bemerkungen:

S. 6. Die gedruckte Vorlage hat im ersten Takt für die Fagotte einen Bogen vom tiefen *C* zum *des*, nämlich

der in den mitgehenden Violoncellen und Kontrabässen fehlt. Auch die von Raffs Hand herrührende Partiturabschrift hat dieses angebundene Sechzehntel in den Fagotten – vermutlich eine Schreibreminiszenz von den vielen Stellen, wo das Motiv tatsächlich so erscheint. Hier muß es wohl gestoßen sein.

S. 9, 1.—6. Takt hat die gedruckte Vorlage folgende (vielleicht von Raff stammende) ungebräuchliche Notierung des 3. und 4. Horns im Baßschlüssel

die nach der üblichen Schreibweise so

lauten muß. Das Gleiche wiederholt sich auf S. 33, 3.—6. Takt und S. 35, Takt 4 bis S. 37, Takt 2.

S. 24. Die gedruckte Vorlage hat schon bei den letzten drei Achteln des 4. Taktes in den I. Violinen die Angabe »arco«. Diese durch den Vergleich mit der analogen Stelle auf S. 28, letzter Takt als fehlerhaft sich ergebende Vorschrift ist auf die nicht ganz genaue Schreibweise in Raffs Kopie zurückzuführen, die das *arco* zu früh, links neben »*f*« hat.

S. 34. Das im letzten Takt über dem Achtel (2. Taktviertel) in den Bläsern stehende Marcatozeichen (>) fehlt bei der analogen Stelle auf S. 15 und kommt überhaupt bei keinem der gleichartigen Rhythmen vor. Doch muß es als authentisch angesehen werden, da Liszt es eigenhändig mit roter Tinte hineinkorrigiert hat.

* * *